Parables & Myths

Other Books by Climbing Sun

Sun, William. *The Blue* (a novel). 310 pp. River Sanctuary Publishing, 2013.

Climbing Sun, William. *Sundances: Prose Poem*s. 86 pp. River Sanctuary Publishing, 2017.

Available from:
riversanctuarypublishing.com
Amazon.com
...and other online retailers

See also *www.climbingsun.com*

Parables & Myths

Poetry

by Climbing Sun

Parables & Myths
Copyright 2018 by William Climbing Sun

All rights reserved. No part of this book may be reproduced without permission of the author.

Cover and interior design by River Sanctuary Graphic Arts
Cover artwork by Melanie Gendron
"Magic Circle" images on title page and divider pages by Melanie Gendron
Illustrations on pages 13, 19 and 54 by Jo Bainbridge Cobbett

ISBN 978-1-935914-82-2

Additional copies available from:
riversanctuarypublishing.com
Amazon.com
www.climbingsun.com

Printed in the United States of America

RIVER SANCTUARY PUBLISHING
P.O. Box 1561
Felton, CA 95018
riversanctuarypublishing.com
Dedicated to the awakening of the New Earth

To the Mystery

and all fortunate beings

who dwell within it.

May our gratitude extend

beyond our inner and outer borders.

Acknowledgements

Fundamental credit for this first collection of my poems in verse form is gratefully given to Mort Marcus, now deceased, yet joyfully remembered. His influence continues to affect virtually everything I write.

I am beyond grateful to Jo Bainbridge Cobbett for allowing me to include the exquisite, long-lost drawings that accompany several of the poems. We embarked on a collaboration in the late 1970's which went dormant as we morphed careers and lost contact for a time. For a glimpse both of Jo's amazing ability to movingly complement a poem, as well as her capturing of the soul of yours truly, have a long look at *Come Back Ravenous*.

My two editors, Annie Elizabeth Porter and Katherine Ziegler, have again provided the thought-provoking insights and thorough scrutiny that have made these poems shine with a far higher polish than they otherwise would have expressed had I remained in my comfortable vacuum.

Lastly, I owe homage to whichever Entity, Conglomerate, Force, or Intelligence created the cosmos—especially the earth—with all of its diversity and awe-inspiring life forms, light shows, vistas, sounds, fragrances, and textures which provide an incessant source of poems.

Contents

Introduction..1

Part 1: **Parables**

In My Cave...5

The Writer 6

lust at the farmer's market 7

Recycling Center at Impact 8

Neverland 10

mortar and pestle..................................12

while picking fruit 14

the iron lady..15

two-youth sanctuary.............................17

The Blush of Joy.....................................19

Departure of the Young........................21

flight of the inspired cynic 23

on responsible vagabonding...............25

evolution of them..................................27

Image Therapy..28

peace is almost too easy 30

mansion earth...32

remember the question 34

Part 2: Myths

- the empty field theory 39
- lotus inc 41
- from the swamp 43
- one flesh 44
- lucky electrons 46
- the slowing 48
- A Small Appeal Inside the Pentagon 51
- Come Back Ravenous 53
- on swimming 55
- a tale of two plates 57
- The Bubble Game 58
- One Tear 61
- About the Author 63
- About the Illustrations (Jo Bainbridge Cobbett) 63

Introduction

Parables. The word evokes everything from the metaphor-rich teachings of Jesus, to Plato's allegories, to Cherokee legends, to the sayings of Confucius. Sages, humorists, scribes, and common folk in every culture have added wisdom in the form of succinct stories designed to illustrate some universal truth, moral lesson, or ethical principle. Though they may not describe their work as parables, any number of modern poets such as Mary Oliver, Billy Collins, Courtney Walsh, and Gary Snyder are writing them. This is one of the noble tasks of poets everywhere: to observe, to open the inner ears to Wisdom, to corroborate her instruction, then to personalize, sculpt, and re-broadcast the insights gained.

Many of the pieces in the Parables section originated out of whimsy, and ended up saying what they wanted to say. Fortunately I listened—although for every one I "heard," three remain languishing in my unfinished file. Two-thirds of these pieces were born during my 22-year run of guiding Montessori Junior High students to write their own truths, musings, and perceptions. It comes as a shock to discover this fact years after my last poetry class. At some point I may choose to develop this realization into a parable of its own loosely titled: *What the Students Taught*. So as you ingest these offerings, realize that they are in effect distillations of what was created while under the influence of these bright, diligent students.

Myths are archetypal stories that have evolved over centuries. So why categorize the group of poems herein as myths when they do not fit the definition? Is this kind of writing going outside the bounds of poetic license and if so, what gives even a longtime poet the right to call his poems myths?

In the larger sense, myths have evolved as a way of bringing comfort or insight to human beings seemingly caught in the gristmill of natural phenomena, death, afterlife, and most especially, the dramas and traumas of life itself.

Myths also seek to explain the origins of the earth and cosmos-at-large and the placement of the tribe or culture within the greater whole. In other words, these are attempts—however noble or feeble—to explain the supernatural and the mystery of existence.

So one day I woke up and noticed that for some years I'd been writing myths. This seemed as natural to me as eating and sleeping. I'll not speculate on where these "came from," (which would itself be a mythical exercise) except to say that in the spirit of myth-refiners down through time, if these bring a measure of solace, reassurance, understanding, or perhaps an enhancement of your place in the cosmic drama, then I will have succeeded.

Part 1

PARABLES

In My Cave

In my cave I saw an oracle study the rocks and send a morning out to play atop the shingles of a gold city. I found myself at the market place looking into the eyes of a flower seller.

I leaned in too far and fell into a moss tabernacle where the queen was a green lily and the king a violet rose. Then kneeling to kiss their soil, I spilled through my lips and followed a bronzing brook toward a great hammering.

Just then a royal trout fell into step beside me. My voice said, "Sir fish I am beginning to parch. Perhaps a drip of your insight would unthirst me."

"Your parchment shall be your mirage *and* your oasis," he silenced.

In time we heard the mist from a singing fountain and were expected to strum the spectrum we found effervescing at the center of each bit of mist. We noticed that of all the colors, not one was able to sound the same.

"Watch closely!" said the fish. To my amazement, he gathered the fountain into a feather pen and placed it in my hand. Then he knelt beneath a great parchment tree where I bundled him with the bark—to bring him here—though, when I open the bundle, only the wrappings remain.

Yet that place is not unreachable. I am there whenever the pen decides to sing.

The Writer

She ponders her next book.

In three hundred pages only she could weave together record temperatures, a coal strike, and a two-faced princess whose secret the CIA cannot uncover.

The hero's heart is caught in a gloomy trap brought on by the mania of trying to live forever. He remains unaware that the ensuing holographic wheel of fire embedded in his chest is consuming his vitality.

He becomes addicted to watching a colony of chimpanzees for clues to the repeating malfunction of his prototype robot—the one upon which he's risked his family fortune.

At night he reads about dim white dwarfs to confirm his theory that control of heaven's light has fallen to blind angels.

He is released from self-imposed repression when his wife's eyes accidentally behold a rising blue moon. As if by Divine Intervention, her hunger for immortality finally matches her husband's.

Just when it appears the tables have turned, the twenty-something subversives next door (employed by the two-faced princess to sabotage his robot) are bent on releasing psychedelics into the water supply which proves to be an almost welcome distraction from a larger evil involving coal-power-plant–emission-induced memory loss, classified antidotes, and accompanying nightmares about hallucinating angels.

Only one ending is certain: the Writer's book will keep others company.

She will remain alone.

lust at the farmer's market

eye contact is the key
we keep the talk factual   logical at first
then begin slipping in musical words:
     numinous   salacious   opalescent

let us agree to ignore the succulent onions
while we pet those starving phantom dogs
gnawing each others' lumbar discs

in front of the wild honey
we have to allow the chaos
to underscore our howls and stutters
letting double signals slip
off the overweight parts of our tongues

a fantasy is not a wholesome idea
instead   you be the analyst
i'll be the dehydrated client

don't even try to pretend
your right leg is attracting my left leg

let us distract our cravings
with tasteful reflections:

     every vendor's bright eyes reflect
     the wider world running on pain

     only the racy rebels are joyful   anymore

     but their delight   like everyone else's
     is as temporary
     as these deep-rooted hungers

Recycling Center at Impact

He was an ex-heavy milk drinker from the Midwest. She was visiting permanently from the smog belt.

They met at the can smasher.

He admired the primalish silt under her nails. She perceived a tidal tap dance lapping in and out of his hands.

Finally she paraphrased the intensity:

> "The masses are in agony.
>   Soon they'll be burning their check books
>   for warmth."

> "Sooner they'll be struggling to unblister their lungs,"
> he counter-predicted—offering to crush her tin foil.

She tossed over a burlap bag, half filled with gritty metallic remains.

> "These are very old cola cans
>   gifted me by a vacant lot!"

> "Hasn't the last vacant lot's charm been amputated?"

Too late he realized his Armageddons were sadly slapstick. He wished he could sniff them offstage into that dank cubby hole below his throat.

Below that, what few scraps of eternal child he'd planned to display, shrank and began withdrawing into a wad of untieable knots.

She remained unaged by his process.

        "At least one vacant lot prospers.
        By a distant river I found it. Drowsy—
        as if its owner left it in charge
        of the three o'clock breeze."

"How can you afford to travel that freely?"
he cross-examined, lobbing a thick blue bottle
into the glass bin.

        "The state pays me to discover
        why people seldom smile anymore."

"Why don't they?"

        "Because the end could come
        this abruptly."

Neverland

Average day in the life:

Before work, I went over Niagara Falls in a kayak. Then I solved the company's primary crisis by hiring our rivals to handle our toughest account. To celebrate, our legal team flew to Maine for lunch but couldn't land because of a toxic lobster bloom.

Shaken to the spine, I called my ex to discuss our addiction of inhaling horror movies most every night. We concluded these movies remind us of our false feelings for each other. We ended the call with a mutual blood-curdling scream followed by my vintage whimpers and her wicked laugh.

Back at the office, I overheard some co-workers plotting to sabotage the lyrics of a rap group. I ratted on them. Within minutes the pest-control people showed up.

Suddenly desperate for nutrition, I raided the window box garden on the 56th floor. Window cleaners called the shrinks. We all had a nice chat. They called it negotiation.

All I really wanted was a chance to do something singular. They obliged by letting me toss myself over the side. I'm writing this in mid air. I'm OK as long as I don't look down. They're OK as long as I don't look up at them and wave. The world is OK as long as I keep my eyes open, and never land.

mortar and pestle

last year   little mattered

now i crush as many sweet seeds
as i find   and bury them   in cakes
i leave on the sill to cool

the jays flash down
tearing in vain at the hot dough
and squawk away   without taste

passing quail peck it and run
without praise

but one bold sparrow watches from the lilac
until the others withdraw
then glides in like my own soul   to feast and inspire

you see i stumbled one dusk
upon an oak-studded plateau
and felt a hundred wings rush my head
on their dance around the canyon

i heard urgency in that fluff
deeper than the everyday message
in their feathers

these were sparrows
ordinary in color   normal in feature
with a speed of sharks   and heart of ponies

one grazed my hair
absorbing a speck of scent
after which her flock refused her

she accepts her fortune
and tells me all she knows
in exchange for the cake

i'll give you all her insight someday
after you've been touched
by this desperate earth
and dare to crush your wildest gifts
then submerge them in your creations
to lure me in
to be fed

while picking fruit

consider the peach tree
she plunges into darkness
with ten million fingers
collects tarnished pieces of light
billows them up through her bones
like a fountain
fashions them into those perfect golden globes
then   when the right wind blows
drops them into our lives like messengers
from places we forget to go

a mother's and fathers body forms a tree
its fruit   the sunlit sons and daughter moons
who spin across our days and nights like jewels
on a never-ending necklace

look at your own life
if you find one of those luminous strands
hung around you
know you truly are a tree and know
your fruits are born
no different from those inbound spirits
who pick
you

the iron lady

her hair   an unborn-rain color
lips   two festivals merging
eyes   a double moonrise

her fingers   in winter   sift firewood ash
to rescue   spent nails from common burial

her feet   in spring   search and re-search   back alleys
overused shorelines   forgotten lots
where her hands   scavenge
rusted bolts broken blades small tangles of wire

upon the strike of midsummer's noon
her whole-body
charges to the heart of its garden
armed with a double-handled digger

twelve holes later   under stinging shower
she circles and begins a wait
for the new   of the next moon

at that exact moment by lantern light
she feeds in her yearly steel-crumb collection
backfills each hole with drooling soil
then celebrates with raisins
and juicy pitted prunes

she nourishes the earth   she must
because some men

      have bled its metal out
   she nurses the earth   she must
        because   she must

so she reaches a fist out to the night
    pulling in a positive charge

then   amused by its sudden gravity   in her chest
    tunnels through her unlit house
      all the way to the mirror
       to laugh   at the image
  of a servant who drops to her knees
         on warm mornings
and fingers the globe   like a rosary bead

two-youth sanctuary

yesterday after the wind
i went yelling
along the creek

the knife blade you found
was loose in my fist

i hid in that spot
where we caught the sun
dipping in a chalice of limbs

there i called the moss
to claim that blade back

i heaved it so hard
the cardinals beat away
leaving a ruby feel to the air

then came that song we love
from the storm lady
who watches this place

i had her promise
we could keep the world turned
mild side out

she made me lean over a hole in the creek
make a deal with my face
and say i'd believe

we need that blade
if creation ever lets someone else
retrieve it

then the clouds hammered out a shower
to pound it farther into the ground
than rust

suddenly the sun shot through
and glanced off the water
landing deeper in me than diamond light

i had to smile
at the blindness it brought—and the rarity
as my face alone felt bright as you
when your eyes get wide

...the job of the poet is to scream the beauty! —Mort Marcus

The Blush of Joy

Standard men will say, "The blush of joy is merely an inflammation of the brain." But I've seen it on the faces of blue ducks in yellow forests in Asia. I've seen it during my pilgrimages to the shocking blossoms in Death Valley. I've seen it on the skins of people who harness the sun's gusto.

On hikes through the clouds, I've seen the green teeth of the earth nibble on the sky's azure face. I've seen the eucalyptus, trunks like chocolate fiber, swaying against a tangerine sea backlit with light so jagged, some crazy queen must have dashed her mirror to the ground in jealousy on her way to explore the mountains of shadow.

I've felt the earth's lips tremble as she let out her untapped sorrow. I've felt steel shoes crush her meadows and witnessed teenage trees sentenced into the fire. The world seems to be wobbling more than ever.

Darkness has its fascinations. But this has not stopped me from hugging the rocks. Has not stopped me from bathing in starlight showers. Has not stopped me from sitting on a shore at midnight, drenched in the moon's almost eternal amber. Has not stopped me from watching the water wink to the deer who pause at the pond.

As I awaken to the soft sound of frost shimmering on the grass, to the sweet saltiness of aquamarine walls playing tag with me, to the display of that great fireball dancing onto a plum-colored horizon, my inner whisper declares again, in full awe, to Creation:

What an artist you are!

Departure of the Young

Even though we kept silent   we were filled with a deep quaking
At this he threw his legs off his bunk   and held us as if we were children
Like a comet orbiting the sun   he stared at a map of the world
A moment later he spoke:

                 Take me to the main road
                 I'm going out to the corner islands
                 I'll set sail in a little boat
                 I need no extra provisions

                 For sustenance I'll take
                 a heaping basket of infrared light
                 and a canteen of refreshing dreams

I've never heard you talk like this before   I said

                 I'm off to examine the passions of mankind
                 off to snare the roaring at the edges
                 of the Seven Wonders

                 I know there is more to life
                 than this vast soaring darkness
                 that haunts my laughter

                 More to life than a plaid bathrobe
                 a warm room and a telephone

But you're always saying how important families are
how they complete the decoration of the tree of life   said mother

> *It's my time to fly off—a solitary bee*
> *who must flutter to paradise's vibration*
> *before I might revisit the hive*

Keep your bile in the little iron vessel you hide
in that crypt
where your turning stomach
meets the nerve path to your tongue
> cried my psyche

He slung his bag over his shoulder
and with one foot out the door
turned beautifully back to speak:
> *Even if you somehow stumble*
> *and drop a good thought*
> *meant for me*
> *I won't judge*

Mother then said:

We will seek to understand
if you will seek to return
filled with even more wonder
after this pure and simple and severe fever
which now consumes you
has taught you what it means
to choose the style of your boundlessness intelligently
lest it become a glamorous shackle
which you may never be able
to choose   to unlock

for Mary Bruggeman of International Falls

flight of the inspired cynic

drenched in the ghostly music
at the headwaters of a grand river
i ask
how loud must god whisper
before wisdom
finally submerges rage

yet looking from this sanctuary
i notice
the continent sitting on its shelf
and the sun
coming out of its cloudy closet

descending to the village
i marvel
because despite alcohol and neon
despite cigarettes and noise
these people look like light and speak
with the transparency
of air

ambling among them
i am startled to detect
their atmosphere holds
as much love as a Venice wedding

passing through the outskirts
i am grateful for the good fortune
to escape this disturbing sacredness

unable to partake in this style of riches
i leave my lip service swirling
in their ears
like the barely audible rage
of their dammed-up river
its soul inundated by too many man-made conflicts
to allow it the freedom to tumble
through the once mystical mist
draped over its forgotten flooded falls

on responsible vagabonding

just as the dog wags its tail
in a way that attacks your heart
you cannot be a vagabond
without fatally affecting the larger culture

you have no doubt danced in a sacred crater
kissed the wet lips of a desert oasis
or safeguarded a lake so immaculate
you have become transparent

those who think they are alive
may brand you as a member
of the living dead

but you are clear
the only stigmas that own you
are the ones you gift to yourself

the thirst you have is a sweet fruit
plucked from translucent trees in some meadow
the pale-faced have yet to penetrate

allow them
because when your exploits become legend
war veterans may end up flinging their medals
or the unrhythmic may discover the drum

allow them
because if they glimpse you repainting a rainbow

or advancing a medicinal form of percussion
party animals may abandon their cages
and corporate rangers their velvet ruts

you   unlike a manikin
possess a furious urge   a trajectory
from which your pure tears proclaim
the blurred edges of your life
are your target   your solace
your sentence

evolution of them

after a minor eternity looking up into the tree
they're still nibbling overripe ground fruit

finally they're reaching up into the tree
groping its pristine offspring

unable to contain their senses
they're shinnying up the trunk like wood eels

in a quest for more encounters
they're passing the fruit by
going hand over hand through the branches

they're waving from the top

with a hand and foot in mid air
they're swaying in the breeze

hopping across clouds
they're hovering over the whole orchard
the full watershed
the entire continent

they're break-dancing on some barren star
squinting back at their planet

almost motionless
they're acting out a somber opera
starring their teeth
about to enter the fabled flesh
of a nectarine

Image Therapy

I stick my mind out the window, lose my grip and tumble onto a poetry trampoline.

By chance I swallow a pair of lightning bugs who try to exit my head from the back of my eyes. Colors blur by at untimable speeds. People laugh in the background.

I hear an anxious valley yell up at a gray mountain that its river is convinced it is dust. I could referee, but the brisk air I breathe lifts me above my private swamp like a child waking from a black-and-white dream.

Two white doves hip-hop in the sky—melodic dots on a blue canvas. They cause me to notice I'm standing in rainbow-stained boots.

Hues of the sunset erupt from a vat of boiled popsicles teetering on the distant edge of the sea. As the sky fabric finally fades, I try to cry—and fail because even though someone is folding up the light, the landscape is not sad.

Then someone else hollers, "Put the used-up day in the wheelbarrow!" At this I can only grin because I now know that judging odd utterances is an advanced form of madness. One must allow that they might turn out profound.

Even as a third party pours black bleach on the sky, causing the uncaring dark to drop like a tightly-knit onyx shawl over my city, I know this is not the end.

I need only distract myself recalling my childhood wonder at counting autumn leaves in an early snowstorm as they spilled from the trees like leaflets out of silver planes.

I need only lock eyes with the illuminated grandmother who occupies the moon as she reflects herself upon a bay infecting it with bliss.

But trust me. All that has gone before is almost normal. Stranger events have captured me—like the rough time I had trying to comb the hairs on a cranky cactus. Or the night I camped in a forest of jagged icicles and dreamed coconut-cream skeletons came to eat them. Or the night I babysat a pack of effervescent toddlers who acquired garnet and hazelnut eyes because they opened a drawerful of moons by mistake.

No, this floating moment is about as far from strange as it is possible to drift.

If it feels like you are caught in an unrhymed, free-verse, word tsunami, remember this:

> One poet's fetish of trying to drown you in the Image Ocean
> is the same poet's way of offering an endless set of rescues
> to help save your brain from a dehydrated fate
> out in the barren plains of logic where even the mirages
> become scorched in the hot coals
> of unattainable perfection.

peace is almost too easy

all you do is reach   reach like a raspberry hunter
reach like a distant aunt bequeathing her estate to the Quakers
stretch like carpenters raising a ridge   singers crying from their guts
old lovers trying a new bed   because peace is easy   all you do is touch

touch every kind of noun
a baby   a great uncle   a maple leaf

kiss your goldfish on the lips
fall in love with paris   or Iceland—it doesn't matter
pick up a twig   a pine cone   a five-dollar bill
now let everything fall through your fingers
touch like tomorrow is doubtful   touch because yesterday never was

peace is easy   all you do is emerge
emerge from nothing's cocoon   like a butterfly-bedecked jet
emerge like you've forgotten your previous three billion emergences

peace is easy   if you contact the awareness in air
if you caress every split second of sunlight   every gray grain of rain
peace will be with you

so approach the roulette table like a mystic   bet like you'll win a windfall of breath
declare yourself a champion   for even if the ball always lands on black
peace is your default medallion

      so propose to turquoise   she's always listening
    decode the hypnotism in silver   he's tired of holding it in
    dip the tax man in platinum until his attitude shines

        and when the powers come for you
    extend like a heron over your symbolic lake
        bank into your most majestic turn
  glide above the semiprecious earth like love itself
           all to teach the ground troops
  how easy peace can be   especially in that instant
while the bullet they've marked for you   still belongs to the sky

"in my father's house are many mansions…" —*Jesus Christ*

mansion earth

fully inhabit this holy mountain morning
allow its pastel spell to pump up my lungs
hyperventilate like an oxygen addict
breathe upon my demons
until they animate   roar them into corners
                              crush their shells
                              or blow them up to burst
                              into so many jokes   now

run breathing where
serene trees speak
without volume   run entranced where deer
                              high on some young bud
                              foxtrot among exotic ferns
                              who mistake themselves for bengals
                              waltzing   now

run color-hungry
where maroon mushrooms
hailing from pluto
assume they are statues
born on filigreed floors
all dissolving into bluegrass and fuchsia   run serenading
                                                          where van goghs and monets know
                                                          and picassos and dalis dream
                                                          they are notes
                                                          on some symphony score   now

run in flamboyance posing
where michaelangelos expose
and raphaels and berninis conduct

the nth movement of
divine opus number nothing   run bedazzled
                                                              where the path expands onto sand
                                                             embracing breaking waves
                                                             inviting pilgrims to be baptized
                                                             standing on water   now

forever run young
where sunrise is your drug
moonlight your concubine
and your footprints   surrounded by sanctuary
follow you as a multitude of replicas of lives
so fully lived   you cannot
remember   who you were   when
before   became   now

Dynamic Meditation, circa 2002
Mt. Madonna, CA

remember the question

come with me on a walk
over the verge of the apparent world

trees here talk back
streams seethe like melted stars
orchids misbehave like weeds
common rocks confess their longing
to aspire to pure quartz

katydids and cicadas rage in sync with drums
we seldom hear but whose echo we sense

a half an hour has no meaning
while you are held for ransom by a waterfall's dance

an accident has no impact
if you can convalesce next to a cobalt ocean

even a bee sting in this region can lead to rejoicing

listen

overhear the growl in your belly
tell you it's a mere metaphor for a craving
created centuries before you came to know
the soil here is spiked
and the air is barely able to maintain
this is no patriotic picnic
no designer daydream

this is all about over-imbibing your own breath
until your rainbow-scented sweat
becomes a truth serum in reverse
making you admit you are blindfolded
and when handed the proverbial stick you get the cosmic joke:
your very existence is the only gift in the piñata

whether you think this is enough is the question

so scale a sacred cliff face
or plunge into that wet emerald basin
waiting to claim you

it's all breathtaking
all yours

don't just grin   don't just smile
catch your echo laughing

and let the madness in that laugh tell you
the unending repetition of the question is everything

Part 2

MYTHS

the empty field theory

what if the beginning was a shiny nugget
packed with music so thick   jammed with love and turmoil so intense
every sound   every substance   every event that would ever be
every emotion that would ever emerge   lie coiled inside it

what if all colors were compressed to specks
all future motion frozen on the surface   all stories fused into one word
every experience of every atom were bunched more densely
than a septillion melted galaxies—all distilled into a thimble-sized nugget

what if the nugget were sitting on some dusty shelf
in a vacant hut   in a land
where day is a dream and night is the same as nothing

what if it were waiting for the caress
of a wandering adept
who   holding it tight in his palm
would breathe into it
across a tongue rich with symbols
through lips blistered with the spirits of orbit

an architect adept
enchanted to his flash point
by ideas of spheres and helixes and jagged spires
by notions of aromas and textures and ecstatic tastes
all huddled in the nugget he found on the shelf
in the vacant hut in the land
where day is eternal and night surrounds everything else

we may never know
if it was he   or his more brilliant sister
who on purpose actually hurled that nugget into the empty field
where nothing had ever grown

what we do know is
no one says that   about the field   anymore

lotus inc

lotuses often dream
about the rich indigo tint given off
by zealous muscles shuddering
during workouts in the summer surf

lotuses sometimes dream
about flamboyant flamingoes
with glistening lips
who wish for women
to bathe with them

lotuses also dream
about peach trees who speak: *yellow food is essential*
for the human animal to flourish

though from the back alleys
the treasure hoarders rant: *when summer is gone*
we'll bottle the glisten out of the lips
the joie de vivre out of the peaches
even the shudders out of the muscles
and remake the world gray again

yet lotuses
shimmer from their pools
and tune to the multi-hued channel
where the season nightly resets to early june
because in this trance
lotuses and lotuses only
thrive in a land beyond the money shrubbery

lotuses and lotuses only
shape the divine sales curve
transmit the ultimate kiss
and enliven the sweet allure
that drenches all heaven-sent flesh

from the swamp

let's re-spin the continuing myth

a mammoth vagabond lump
struck our globe
that era when dinosaurs wore the crowns

dust splashed into orbit
and those big king-and-queen beasts
saddened by lack of sun
sobbed into the swamps to shiver no more

ages later dust dropped
skies shined again
carbon chains rearranged
incubation recurred
then from the waters we hatched
to forage our way to their thrones

now in soiled royal robes
in paralytic chariots we sit
stalking the wild sound byte
yet reach in need for tender planet flesh
but watch instead our insulting selves
slapping the planet
sending up another   and another   and another   insidious dust
as fast fattens the artificially inseminated landscape
at our backs   as we   stumbling up
to the sudden rising edge of father swamp
utter our foreboding to an uncertain sky
and shiver like little carbon copies
of some lineage
too big to vanish again   simply

one flesh

some say
we were once detained
like a formless puff
in god's belly

if that's true
we were as bored
as a one-syllable rhyme

if that's true
surely our voice revolted
as one almost angry
almost ecstatic   scream

if that's true
somewhere in the fury   we forgot
we are mother and midwife of matter:
its fetus   its parasite   its host
its companion

so let us wear the moment
like a baby's skin

let us love like thunderstorms
in a cage

let us treat each tree
like an original cezanne

and for god's sake
let us gaze out   as god's eyes
at this wounded world
made of one puff   one note
one blessed flesh

lucky electrons

all particles are not created equal

some are doomed to drift
in the bleakest loneliest darkest regions
of the most nebulous sectors
in creation
where their annihilation
by bursting stars and black holes
is merciful

the chosen ones comprise
the coronas of suns
heads of comets
polar crowns of planets
and last an infinite instant

the chosen ones compose the skin
on the fingers of musicians
the inner thighs of dancers
and tongue tips of lovers
until they expire
as blips of unconditional love

the chosen ones coexist with daybreak and dusk
tumbling like gymnasts
in the atmospheres
around planets

the chosen ones cavort within chlorophyll and enzymes
                in the food chain
                   until they
        like others of their ilk before them
             convert to burnt calories
              and make the equal leap
                    to light

the slowing

i.

a million years back
we walked with our souls in a garden world
where each orchid opened its song
to a diamond sky

we swam in lakes
so full of grace
there was no knowing
where skin stopped
and liquid sapphire began

we had temples
with windows
that looked out on infinity
and stairways that ached
for the cadence of our footsteps

we slept under stars so excited
by the wild silence
our dreams melted into our days
like honey flowing back to a hive

a million years before
we felt the planet harbor us
as it would
any chorus of temporary angels

ii

don't bother to shelter yourself:
i pitch no sermon
about the demise of the sky
no lament
for the saddening of rivers
no manifesto
on the fading of wildlife

don't bother to brace yourself:
i promise to keep you from the mental maze
where belief seeps in to spread its infection

iii.

forgive me if i sin:
i find no morals in the sun's outpouring
in the child's smile
or the rose's resplendence

where is the opinion
in the hungry hawk's dive
the lion's leap
or the cedar's cling to the cliff

show me the idea
that can improve a moonrise
enhance the symphony in a blizzard
or cause more joy in a dolphin

iv.

we are here
a million years on and counting

can we remember
when delicious nourishing air
was enough

can we remember
when a simple sip of water
sent us hurtling
into pools of halleluias

a million years on
how can we forget
you and i are nothing less
than exhaled breath
from the lung of some nebula's body

how can we forget
in that instant when we taste
the kiss of a loved one—or a raindrop—
we sample the spirit
embedded in everything

when we really slow our drama down
how can we forget
we are the chosen dwellers
on a miraculously turning sphere
in no other moment
but the one   sacred   free   now

A Small Appeal Inside the Pentagon

In what seems like another life I said, "I am finished with this valley!"

But on my last walk while passing a bomb-shaped boulder I stumbled onto a stairway that stretches up toward the center of the sun.

Looking out everything is lit: spires and tree tips, icicles and irises, whitewater and wine, even the sparkling sword that is infinite night. Enthralled beyond all control, I hurl myself off the stair onto its cold blade.

To my fascination I don't die exactly but am thrust through a portal into a solemn carnival where I am an only clown whose antics are so un-sad I am captured by roving, carefree space beings who detain me as the centerpiece of a painting on the top-floor-office wall of some pentagon general who at this moment, while staring at my frozen, hypnotic grin, realizes he must call off the global air strike lest it upset the balance of grief in the galaxy.

When I set out I had no plan—no inkling of being trapped beneath this glass sheet. Still, my paralyzed smile is an ache I accept—a small offering toward that joy craved by the many.

I foresee that when this building burns, the ashes from the painting where I dwell will enrich whatever—hopefully utopian—landscape emerges.

If you are listening, please set this five-sided nightmare—where I hang—on fire.

I would but my fingers are not even in the picture. It's as if I remember them but in a curious way no longer need them.

If you found out your smile could only emanate from behind glass in a solitary tower so much more hellish than the sweet delirium to which you were so innocently ascending, perhaps you would become explosive.

I dream about resuming my journey to the center of the sun. Though if truth be told, the promise of dubious bliss is more self-deceptive than this certainty of existing as an influential force. A small beacon. Unassailable. Behind glass. On a wall. Like a page in a book. That might be read by some starved yet potentially caring soul. An image that might be pondered by some hardened warmonger who suddenly cannot take another step in the sad and fatal direction he is leading the naive.

In 1807, Irish author Isaac Weld wrote:
[Americans have an] "unconquerable aversion to trees."

Come Back Ravenous

Once it lived upon the pure wind of spirit frolicking from sun to sun. One eternal spring it was stunned by the drone from a blue and barren Mother. Her quirky climate happened to match its own whimsical rhythms.

So it tucked itself away in her crust until she shook with an urge to push. Out it sprouted, up it sprung. Her adopted child, self resolute now fixed on but one sun—yet daring to wear her planetary air.

Its first breath turned leaf-green. Then came a strong cough that chased glaciers away and began to make this land into a great jade and emerald maze.

Everywhere it crept, at a crawl it spread, into her hollow places, up her crested breasts inspiring itself by playing with perspective. It got so glad it ran through canyons, skipped over cliffs, hopped across swamps.

A spirit myself, I admired, trying to follow, hurrying my dance to a verge where the ancestors and I overheard it laugh down a valley, tickle a river, torture a gorge.

I swear it seduced a storm, showed off to a lake, burned its own fingertips on purpose. I think I glimpsed it lumber up a ridge, split up on a divide, then dive toward both coasts.

I tracked its verdant footprints west but there for some reason, it just faded into sand and brush. By the time I overtook, much of it had vanished in a great puff of grief. By some logic or panic beyond my grasp, it retreated or fell back just under the dust.

I almost smell it. If I squint, then set my senses adrift, I see its remains on display in untamed places. On then and farther to inner stillness I will track its thin apparition even if that means I squat in pain until I stomach its loss. I sense I must endure the scorch-happy bands' misdeeds with a bit less bitterness. I must somehow forgive those who have charred this child with their chemical packs of matches.

Even if that means I—bent double from having to eat the deeds of mean-eyed people—keep craving a wild, wild enough to devour me with this prayer still in my mouth:

Great Mother, trust me with another forest! Come back ravenous!

on swimming

some say this globe is an ancient mother
but she's really a raved-about babe
with the best complexion in the galaxy

all the man-planets can't go retrograde
when they know she's excited
by those other celestial sinners—
the distant starry ones— who toast her
with their hot intoxicating flickers

she might set off a little heat lightning
just to string them along

but when those closer bodies exert
their nasty gravitational attractions
she does respond steamily: a tempest   tempting a desert
                                          a tornado   whipping a prairie
                                                     a typhoon   massaging a reef-freckled sea

she does respond easily
to that nearest young sun
who flares his stuff
glancing advances off her lakes
and snowy mountain tips
while she fantasizes with an avalanche   an ice thaw   a geyserous burst

sometimes
if venus steals the magnetic rapture
that saturn or jupiter exude her way

she might choose to act like a cooled lava flow
until mars admires her coastlines
or neptune says
"earthy baby   i need your bluest blush"
then she'll let herself
feel these blissful emissions
penetrate her ozone
and caress her weather
causing downpours
where fluids run off her rocks
swell her streams   rush her rivers   rise her tides
treating each creature
lucky enough to plunge below her surface
to the same ecstasy   she expresses
swimming through
each elixir-rich
eros-laden
jewelry-case moment
in reciprocal deep-space
intercourse

a tale of two plates

almost always in some form of foreplay:
their hills stiffening   canyons contracting
cosmic rays bathing their backsides
snow massaging their shoulders
business tickling as usual
every crevice flexed
each nerve ending on the edge
pulse beats   each one a long week
serious but slow breathing between pre-peak experiences
until   uh a uh a uh
a rush to rumba with that adjacent yet estranged plate
to scrape jagged navels   to steal a predestined clinch
a quintuple multi-megaton hug
all to assume new poses in the oldest of yogas
and re-squeeze the co-squeezer
until the evolving verse becomes a legend
which oozes out through some dreamt-up coast dweller:

one more lurch around this whirling world
one more slip toward the instant
some alien asteroid will baste mother egg
like a hurtling sperm

one more tectonic step
one more motion-filled moment
under the briefly-stable sun

one more squeal of geologic delight
one more leap a millimeter into the willing wind
and for a few tensionless seconds
to caress immensely
and forget the pressures of centuries

The Bubble Game

What if some teacher you trust said:

"Today we shall solve the riddle of existence:

Assume for an instant the universe is just a large jar of bubbles floating in an exhaled breath so ancient its source cannot be traced.

Long ago transparent creatures sprung from the bubbles and began to dance on them to celebrate roundness and pigment and temperature.

The creatures soon realized they too were built of bubbles—tinted globes so small and empty they had to form organisms with eyes just to spy on their own uniqueness.

Then because its nature is to amuse, spirit decided to hide itself in all the empty spaces inside and between the bubbles which rub each other—or simply spin contentedly on their own axes.

Then came the turning point: a tap on the cosmic skin, a quick turn, the widening inner eyes looking square into the source—all staring into a very large dream which contained all possible dreams.

Some organisms tamed the dreams and logic was born—a flat antidote to the addicting curvature of the dreams.

This is where the record is blurred. We know there must have been a conference.

Perhaps on a centrally located bubble—perhaps no specific bubble—as communication in that celestial season was immediate, completely shared, infinitely grasped.

In a blink it was offered and decided that this bubble-infested, sprung-from-nothing, real-life animation would be a game. A great Game with a field of never-ending length and players feeble and rugged, dull and bright, thriving and destitute, murderous, euphoric, disinterested, hyper-excited.

Everyone able to play every position. Everyone able and willing to fail, to triumph, to almost seize immortality—or nearly embrace absolute nihilism.

What is the objective, you ask?

To remember the sweetness of the source from which flows the weakest amoeba, the wickedest grizzly, the stoniest mountain, the dizziest star. To remember this symphony so vividly, so collectively, it causes the Game itself to ricochet off eternity for a stretched instant.

And the method for achieving such instances?

Adjust your inhales until your interior bubbles vibrate to a tender frenzy releasing their entombed spirit. To reach this resonance you must assist others in their reaching. To assist, perchance to coax. Never to force, never to trick.

Some rebelled against this rule, becoming so adept at pressure, they wrote it down in symbols. The stronger ones made the weaker ones memorize the writings, instead of teaching them to record their own pictures, their own musings, their own fascinations.

Thus the weaker ones fell way inside the Game and lost their free rhythm. Some struggled through ages to regain it, eventually recalling the textures of central pieces of their distant transparent selves. These were the lucky and the few.

Painstakingly the Game advanced.

The strong broke into a cornucopia of factions, all vying for dominance. Some of the weak deluded themselves into thinking they were strong and stepped onto one-way treadmills from which escape is never guaranteed.

Under the mantle of sport, some of these invented war—which at once spawned peace-wagers. Others created crime. Many more tried on the heavy cloak of boredom. Others brewed up the artistry which set the cloak afire. While others took up pens and instruments causing tsunamis and temblors and bona fide hallucinations within audiences—all under the guise of the Game.

Part One of the Game is succeeding. At last count, five point eight billion have totally forgotten the destination—let alone the origin.

Yet from the sand mandala makers in the monasteries of Tibet, to the tribal fire dancers of Africa, to the Aboriginal rhythmic dreamers of Australia, to the posh patio dwellers above the traffic jams of the American West, to the simple servants of other humans, handfuls of the entranced have almost remembered—a few claim they've never forgotten—that the key is hidden in the smile—or the sigh—of some player in the next seat. That an answer is broadcast by a singer in the next button you punch—or in some random suggestion in a lecture. Or a line of dialogue on a screen. Or in an out-of-time moment when a gong is sounded. Just as surely, that last line of a child's poem—or a mother's lullaby—holds the next clue.

And like a massive arch of bubbles spanning the gorge of emptiness, everyone oddly yet necessarily bonds to hold up the next moment for everyone else's next move—in the Game.

For your homework, pump up your inner bubbles until they burst out and blow you away. And in the process of your becoming a benign explosion, see if you might glimpse the original bubble, have a mad laugh, and expose the Game for what it is: a very wily, personally-tailored, daring, perhaps jubilant way to pass cosmic time without giving in to fatigue, folly, monotony, cynicism, fatalism or that insidious—yet ever beckoning burden—complacency."

One Tear

The Universe is said to have sprung from a single tear. There should be little doubt it fell from the Original Face of Oneness.

Before the tear there wasn't so much a day as a sun-like bundle of pre-belief music: one channel, one volume, one continuous song.

If some forerunner of night was milling around, in its heart it carried awesome anguish of Abraham, condensed presence of Jesus, lucid musings of Buddha, intense blossom of Confucius, vicious beauty of Kali. In its brain it held brutal justice of Zeus, pliable logic of Descartes, brilliant visions of Einstein. To leave these festering in darkness would have been a genuine original sin.

If there was a sky it was colorless, not anti-black, not surprisingly white, yet packed with every color's seed. It was over-comfortable the way it was.

No wonder the Universe sprung from a single tear. Oneness was bored to death. It knew play was its destiny. It had to split something off—to create an unknown known. Though here is the cold, rational, inevitable truth: the inescapability of the shedding of the tear anguished Oneness to its core.

Like a pregnant meteor, when it hit some divine facsimile of ground, the tear self-detonated and gave birth to everything from sparking stars to bejeweled planets, from mineral-rich oceans to frigid moons, from naked cells to mammal families, from angry gasses to sweet human confluence, from nauseous emptiness to refined residence of spirit.

Questions remain: What is the purpose of the tear and what can its residue—within which we dwell—teach us?

When we cry—whether in joy or in anguish—we dissolve into harmony with our essence. When we enter the waters, we remember floating in the tear and are comforted. When we lie down—especially on the earth—we sense we are falling toward home. Tears returning. When we wonder why we are here, we relive the depths of our Original Anticipation. When we dive into life trusting the water is deep enough, trusting our outer-form and inner-dialogue offerings, trusting that the leap itself is the gift—*we* become human tears of joy on the enduring Face of Oneness.

About the Author

Climbing Sun is a world traveler, engineer, teacher, and poet born in Michigan, raised in Ohio, and educated in Florida, who continues to design structures in California and South Florida. He visits the far reaches of the cosmos whenever possible, chasing images to coax onto the printed page.

About the Illustrations

Illustrations for *Mortar and Pestle* (p.13), *Two-Youth Sanctuary* (p.19) and *Come Back Ravenous* (p.54) are "Illuminations" by award winning artist Jo Bainbridge Cobbett. She finds joy in creating drawings, paintings, and murals for individuals, schools and businesses.
Contact her: *jo@movinground.com*

www.ingramcontent.com/pod-product-compliance
Lightning Source LLC
Chambersburg PA
CBHW081356040426
42451CB00017B/3466